Abso
Awful
Adults

Claire O'Brien

Illustrated by Mark Beech

Contents

WHIRLEY COUNTY PRIMARY SCHOOL

Whirley Road,

MACCLESFIELD

OXFORD
UNIVERSITY PRESS Cheshire.

Mr McMeanie,
Minister for Child Control

Mr McMeanie (the Minister for Child
Control) telephoned Mrs Rattle, the head
teacher of Clink Street School.

'All schools should be like yours,' he said.
'There are lots of punishments, no playtimes,
no noise from disgusting children and, best of
all, no colourful pictures on the walls. I hate
colourful pictures.'

'So do I,' said Mrs Rattle. 'I don't allow bright colours in school and I am always trying to think of new rules and punishments. I don't want the children to be happy or they will giggle. I hate giggling.'

'I agree, Mrs Rattle!' said Mr McMeanie. 'I feel sick when children even smile.'

Next, Mr McMeanie telephoned Mr Chumkins, the headmaster at Flowerpot Primary.

Flowerpot Primary was next door to Clink Street School. The children there had an orchard for picnics, hammocks to relax in and a library filled with interesting books. They even spent every afternoon painting.

'Your children are a bunch of softies!' Mr McMeanie shouted.

Mr Chumkins laughed. 'Why don't you come and join our painting party next week?' he suggested. 'We're going to cover the walls with lovely bright flowers.'

Mr McMeanie turned purple with rage. 'Never!' he shouted. 'I hate painting and I hate parties!' and he slammed the phone down.

At Clink Street School, Mrs Rattle made the children scrub the floors and paint the walls grey. There were also very strict rules.

1. NO talking
(not even a whisper).
2. NO smiling, laughing or giggling.
3. NO relaxing.
4. NO making friends.

Mrs Rattle gave out some very nasty punishments, too, like pasting wallpaper over your mouth for the whole day, making you gargle with cold, lumpy gravy, or making you wear a cardboard box on your head.

The worst punishment of all was called The Drench. You were dangled out of an upstairs window in chains and left there all day in the rain.

Nelly and Neville Normington told their parents about Mrs Rattle. Mr and Mrs Normington wrote to Mr McMeanie immediately.

Dear Mr McMeanie

We are very concerned about the treatment of children at Clink Street School. Mrs Rattle is a monster! Please get rid of her and hire a kind head teacher instead.

We want our children to be happy, like the lucky pupils at Flowerpot Primary where lovely Mr Chumkins works.

Yours Sincerely,
Nina and Nigel Normington

(Parents of Nelly and Neville Normington)

Lots of other parents wrote to him too, but Mr McMeanie threw all the letters into his big black bin.

'I must visit Clink Street School,' he decided, 'to make sure Mrs Rattle isn't listening to these silly parents.'

'The school must be perfect when Mr McMeanie arrives,' announced Mrs Rattle at assembly. 'There will be lots of extra jobs to do.'

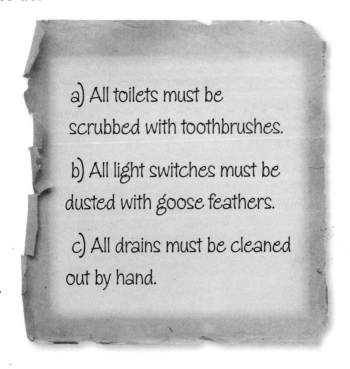

a) All toilets must be scrubbed with toothbrushes.

b) All light switches must be dusted with goose feathers.

c) All drains must be cleaned out by hand.

Nelly and Neville were dusting the light switches. Nelly whispered, 'I think I've got a plan to trick Mrs Rattle.'

'Shh!' said Neville. 'She'll hear you.'

'But listen,' said Nelly. 'If we tell her that *nice* things make us unhappy, she might make us do them.'

'Please don't try it,' said Neville. 'It's so dangerous.'

But it was too late.

'Hello, Mrs Rattle,' said Nelly. 'I *love* dusting.'

Mrs Rattle scowled. 'Is that a disgusting smile I see on your face, you horrid child?'

'Sorry,' said Nelly. 'But I'm just so glad that I'm at this school. Please don't ever make us draw colourful pictures like those poor children at Flowerpot Primary, will you, Mrs Rattle? That would make me so unhappy.'

Nelly's trick worked. She was marched into an empty classroom and given a pile of paper and a pot of felt pens.

'As a punishment for smiling you will draw colourful pictures all afternoon,' said Mrs Rattle.

Nelly pretended to cry until Mrs Rattle slammed the door shut.

'Hooray!' she cheered, and settled down for a lovely afternoon of drawing.

Neville told the others about Nelly's trick.

'Brilliant!' said Freddy. 'Let's all try it.'

'Please be careful,' said Neville, looking worried. But Freddy, Trisha and Jasmine were already waving to Mrs Rattle.

'Hello!' they called.

Mrs Rattle was furious. 'It is against the school rules to be cheerful!' she said. 'Stop it at once.'

'Sorry,' said Trisha. 'But cleaning out the drains is great fun.'

'Please don't ever make us do painting instead, will you?' asked Freddy.

Mrs Rattle immediately ordered them to do painting for the rest of the day.

Neville nudged Jasmine and whispered, 'Remember to sound miserable.'

Jasmine pretended to complain. 'These colours are horribly bright,' she said. 'I'm *so* unhappy!'

'Good!' said Mrs Rattle. 'From now on you will do painting every afternoon.'

And she marched away thinking she had
been very clever.

The children whispered, 'Hooray!' Nelly's
plan was working!

Max and Emily were cleaning the toilets with toothbrushes.

'Good afternoon, Mrs Rattle,' said Emily.

'Stop grinning or I'll make you gargle with cold gravy,' said Mrs Rattle.

'Sorry,' said Max. 'But we can't help it. We just *love* scrubbing the toilets.'

Mrs Rattle's eyes bulged with shock.

'We would hate to read books all day like the children at Flowerpot Primary,' said Emily.

Max nodded and pretended to be sad. 'I would especially hate it if I had to look at books with lots of interesting pictures in them,' he said.

Straight away, Mrs Rattle marched Max and Emily into the room where she had locked away all the books with lovely illustrations.

'As a punishment for enjoying yourselves you will look at these books with interesting pictures for the rest of the day,' she said.

Max and Emily burst into floods of pretend tears until Mrs Rattle had gone. Then they cheered (quietly) and settled down to read.

When Mr McMeanie arrived at Clink
Street School he was horrified. Nelly's plan had
spread throughout the whole school. There
were children drawing, painting, looking at
books and playing games. There was colour
and laughter *everywhere*.

'What have you done?' he shouted at Mrs
Rattle. 'This used to be a good school – grey,
quiet and tidy. You are a disgrace! You're fired!'

Mrs Rattle realized that the children had tricked her. She was *livid*. Mr McMeanie ordered her to pack her bags and leave straight away.

'I will send a new head teacher,' declared Mr McMeanie. He gave an evil laugh. 'My best friend, Mr Hardstone, will be in charge!'

'Oh no!' said Nelly. 'He's worse than Mrs Rattle!'

'But first,' said Mr McMeanie, 'we are going on an expedition where there will be no revolting children to bother us.'

Mr Hardstone and Mr McMeanie liked to go on tough expeditions together. Mr Hardstone held the world records for walking fifty miles in deep snow with bare feet and for leaping over hungry crocodiles while juggling cabbages.

Mr McMeanie and Mr Hardstone set off across the Pacific Ocean in a wooden canoe. As they rowed along they thought up new punishments for Clink Street School. But after a few days, the newspapers reported a tragedy.

DAILY NEWS

Two men swallowed by whale

Whale has indigestion

So that was the end of their plans.

The school was closed for a week while everyone decided what would happen next.

'Who will be our new head teacher now?' Nelly wondered.

'Wait and see,' said her mum, who was writing a letter.

'If they bring back Mrs Rattle,' said Neville, 'I shall run away.'

'Don't worry, Neville,' said his dad, who was sending an email. 'We have a plan.'

When the week's holiday was over, the children discovered the wall between Clink Street School and Flowerpot Primary had been knocked down.

'What's going on?' asked Nelly.

'Perhaps we're not going to have a school at all,' said Neville, looking worried again.

But Mr Chumkins was waiting for them in the hall, smiling and handing out paintbrushes.

'Your parents wrote to the Prime Minister,' he said. 'They asked if we could become one big school. The Prime Minister said yes, so I am going to be your new headmaster.'

The children cheered.

Then Mr Chumkins gave everyone a pot of paint.

'Our first job,' he said, 'is to brighten up these grey walls. After that we'll have a big picnic in the orchard, before relaxing in the hammocks with a good book.'

The children cheered again. Clink Street Flowerpot Primary was going to be the best school ever!

Mrs Rattle couldn't find another job as a teacher. Instead she got lots of tattoos, stole a ship and became a pirate. And a fearsome pirate she was, too!

WANTED!

Captain Rattle,
Terror of the Seas

Of course, she was eventually caught and sent to prison, where she was made to scrub and dust every day ... and all the walls were grey.

Mr Splatter's Dreadful Dinners

The new cook at Crinkle Lane Primary School was called Mr Splatter. His cooking was terrible and everyone was scared of him.

Jenny Brown wrote a description of their school dinners in her diary.

Monday

* Yellow gloop followed by green and orange slop.

Tuesday

* Brown mush followed by slime in a bowl.

Wednesday

* Lumpy grey mash followed by bullet-hard slabs of concrete biscuit.

Thursday

* Dollops of boiled rubbery stuff followed by stale cardboard flapjack.

Friday

* Rotten fish followed by mouldy fruit.

Jenny decided that something had to be done. She took a deep breath and said to Mr Splatter, 'This is really not very nice at all. Could we have something tastier, please?'

'How dare you!' shouted Mr Splatter.

'But it really is awful,' said Colin Granger, who was Jenny's friend.

Mr Splatter turned as red as a boiled beetroot and shouted, 'Be quiet and go away, you revolting children!'

Even the head teacher, Miss Flurry, had had enough. 'The children are right, I'm afraid, Mr Splatter,' she said nervously. 'I really think you could give them something a bit nicer.'

Mr Splatter screamed, 'Get out of my
kitchen!' and threw a rock-hard fruit cake at
Miss Flurry's head. Fortunately she ducked,
but it smashed the clock into little pieces.

The next day, Mr Splatter put loads of
hot chilli powder in everyone's dinner as a
punishment. The children and teachers had
steam coming out of their ears and noses for
the rest of the day.

Jenny was lucky. In the evening her mum always made a delicious meal. There was usually a scrumptious pudding too.

'I'm worried about my friends,' Jenny told her mum. 'Their parents aren't as good at cooking as you are. Sometimes all they have to eat is Mr Splatter's terrible gloop.'

'I'm sorry to hear that,' said Mum, 'but I don't think there's anything I can do to help.'

Mr Splatter's cooking got worse and worse. Jenny made more notes in her diary.

Mr Splatter has started calling everything soup but it is always just a disgusting mash-up of ingredients. We have had:

Monday – Green soup.

Tuesday – Brown soup.

Wednesday – Orange soup.

Thursday – Yellow soup.

Friday – Grey soup.

Jenny tried again. 'Could I have a drink of juice, please?' she asked Mr Splatter.

'No!' shouted Mr Splatter, and he handed Jenny an old bucket. 'Get some puddle water from the playground if you want a drink.'

Jenny and Colin had an idea. They got all the children together.

'We'll stage a protest,' said Jenny. 'Everyone needs to make a big sign.'

They borrowed some materials from the art room and got to work.

At lunchtime the next day, the children marched up to the kitchen window where Mr Splatter would see them. They waved their signs and shouted, 'We want nice food! We want nice food! We want nice food!'

Miss Flurry came out of her office.

'Please, Miss Flurry,' said Colin. 'You have to do something about Mr Splatter.'

Miss Flurry knew she had to be very brave. 'You're right, Colin,' she said. 'After all, I *am* the head teacher. I'm supposed to be in charge.'

She knocked gently on the kitchen door and called, 'I'd like to talk to you, Mr Splatter.'

Mr Splatter opened the kitchen door and poured thick, cold yellow soup over her head.

'Right!' said Miss Flurry, wiping off the mess with a hanky. 'I've had quite enough!'

She knocked on the kitchen door once more. 'Mr Splatter, I'm afraid I must talk to you,' she called.

Mr Splatter came running out shouting, 'Get away from my kitchen!' and chased Miss Flurry around the hall, throwing lumps of mashed potato at her. He chased her all the way back to her office and she didn't dare come out again.

Oh dear! *Oh dear*! *I'm a hopeless head teacher*, she thought. *And I lost my diamond necklace as I was running. What a terrible day*!

Jenny and Colin walked home from school together.

'We must think of another plan,' said Jenny.

Colin suddenly stopped.

'Look, Jenny. Quick! Look in that café.'

'It's Mr Splatter,' said Jenny.

They hid behind a dustbin and watched.
Mr Splatter was scoffing an enormous cream
tea. His table was covered with cakes and
scones and a teapot the size of a pumpkin.

'He's so horrible,' said Colin, feeling angry. 'He feeds us on rubbish and then stuffs his own greedy chops with delicious cake.'

'Let's follow him every day and see what else he's up to,' said Jenny.

On Monday, the children tried to help Miss Flurry find her diamond necklace. They hunted high and low but no one could find it.

After school, Jenny and Colin followed Mr Splatter. He went into Penny's Pizza Place and ate a pepperoni pizza as wide as the table.

Colin took out his camera and snapped a photo.

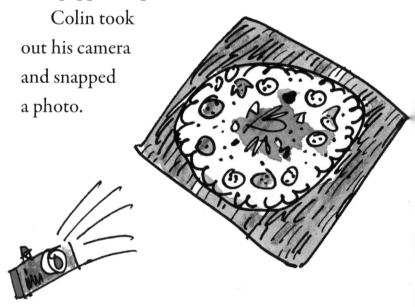

On Tuesday, they followed him to Charlie's Chicken Hut and saw him eat three whole chickens and a slice of creamy strawberry cheesecake.

Colin took another photo.

On Wednesday, they watched Mr Splatter go into Cathy's Cake Shop and buy a massive triple-chocolate-and-toffee-whipped-mousse-cake. Colin took a photo of him as he came out carrying an enormous cake box.

'It makes me so angry,' said Jenny. 'I bet he's spending our school dinner money on all this food.'

On Thursday, they photographed Mr Splatter in Jake's Fish and Chip Shop eating a haddock the size of a whale and a pile of chips as big as his head.

On Friday, they watched him sit down in Monsieur Blanc's Fine French Restaurant. Another man sat down with him. They each scoffed a gigantic blancmange, then Mr Splatter handed something to the other man. Jenny and Colin gasped.

'That's Miss Flurry's diamond necklace!' said Jenny. 'Mr Splatter must've stolen it!'

'Got him!' said Colin, clicking his camera. 'Let's get these photos to Miss Flurry.'

But just then Mr Splatter looked out of the window and saw them. He saw Colin's camera too.

'Stop those kids!' he shouted, and chased after them. The other man ran away.

'Run!' shouted Jenny and Colin. Mr Splatter chased them through the market. He chased them past the library and over the railway bridge.

'This way!' called Colin, pointing to the school.

They climbed in through a window and found Miss Flurry in her office. Colin showed her all the photographs he had taken.

'He's still chasing us,' said Jenny.

'I will call the police immediately,' said Miss Flurry. 'Well done, children.'

Mr Splatter was clattering around angrily in the kitchen.

'I'll teach them a lesson,' he said. 'I'll put chilli powder in the dinner again. And extra-peppery pepper. And lots and lots of monstrously hot mustard!'

He was stirring up the fiery hot gloop when Miss Flurry burst into the kitchen with two police officers.

Mr Splatter tried to climb out of the window, but the children had nailed it shut.

He tried to throw the pan of fiery hot gloop at them but it was too heavy. It spilled everywhere. The splodgy mess went cold and hard and stuck his feet to the floor. The greedy villain was trapped by his own horrible cooking.

Suddenly, Jenny and Colin's parents arrived at the kitchen door.

'You didn't come home!' said Jenny's mum. 'We've been worried about you.'

Mr Splatter was brought out in handcuffs.

'Hooray!' cheered the children.

'This is not Mr Splatter,' said one of the police officers. 'This is Harry Splitter, the notorious jewel thief. We've been looking for him for a long time.'

'Goodness me!' cried the parents.

Miss Flurry smiled. 'Well, that's got rid of him,' she said. 'But who's going to cook the school dinners?'

Jenny thought quickly. 'Why don't you have a little chat with my mum about that?' she suggested.

The next day, Jenny's mum cooked a fantastic feast for the whole school. Miss Flurry wore her diamond necklace. There was orange squash and raspberry cordial for everyone, and the teachers had fizzy lemonade to celebrate.

'Hooray for our brave children!' said Miss Flurry, raising her glass to toast Jenny and Colin.

Later, Miss Flurry asked Jenny's mum, 'Will you stay and be our new cook?'

'Oh, please say yes, Mum,' Jenny begged.

Jenny's mum thought for a moment then said, 'I would love to. When shall I start?'

'Straight away!' said Miss Flurry.

The following week, Jenny wrote in her diary again.

The new school menu is:

Monday – Cheese and mushroom omelette, apple crumble and custard.

Tuesday – Roast chicken, chocolate ice cream.

Wednesday – Spaghetti Bolognese, vanilla cheesecake.

Thursday– Cottage pie, zingy lemon gateau.

Friday – Crispy fish and chips, strawberries and cream.

There will be no more dreadful dinner days at Crinkle Lane Primary School.

From now on, every day will be DELICIOUS DAY!

Mr Peacock, the Very Bright Headmaster

The headmaster at Eric's school was called Mr
Peacock. Mr Peacock liked to wear expensive
suits in bright colours so that everyone noticed
him. His tie and handkerchief always matched
perfectly, and his shoes were always polished.

On Mondays he wore his green suit with yellow stripes.

On Tuesdays he wore his sky blue suit with pink spots.

On Wednesdays he wore his purple suit with white flowers.

On Thursdays he wore his orange and red checked suit.

And on Fridays he wore a white suit with gold triangles and a sparkly bowler hat.

Today was Tuesday – a sky blue suit with pink spots day.

'You children are all far too scruffy!' Mr Peacock announced in assembly. 'We are going to have a new school uniform!'

The children whispered to each other nervously.

'I like the uniform we've got,' said Sally.

'So do I,' said Jason. 'I can carry lots of snacks in the pockets.'

'And the hood is just the right size for my guinea-pig,' said Jessie.

'It looks quite smart, too,' said Eric, 'if we tuck our T-shirts in.'

'Stop that whispering!' shouted Mr Peacock. 'We will have a competition to design the new uniform and there will be a *spectacular* prize for the winner.'

'What do you think it will be?' asked Eric, still whispering.

'It might be book tokens,' said Jessie, who liked reading.

'Or cinema tickets,' said Sally, who loved watching films.

'Free pizzas would be best,' said Jason, who was always hungry.

Instead, Mr Peacock held up a huge photograph of himself. It showed him smiling and wearing his Wednesday suit – the purple one with white flowers.

'The prize will be this *marvellous* picture of me – your handsome, well-dressed headmaster.'

All the girls whispered, 'Yuck!'

The boys pretended to be sick.

'Quiet!' said Mr Peacock. 'The winner will also receive *this*!'

Mr Peacock pulled the corner of a shiny cloth. Underneath it was the most gigantic box of chocolates anyone had ever seen. It was nearly as big as the headmaster himself and was tied up with a gold ribbon. Sally's eyes were popping out like ping-pong balls and Jason was dribbling.

Eric had never won anything before. *It would be amazing if I won those chocolates*, he thought. *If I won I would have a massive chocolate-eating party at my house*!

Mr Peacock continued. 'You are a scruffy bunch of greedy little monsters! If you want to get your sticky fingers on these chocolates you need to stop dribbling and start thinking of ideas for the new uniform!'

No one talked about anything else all day.

chocolates

'Mr Peacock likes bright colours,' said Jessie. 'The winning idea will need to be very colourful, that's for sure.'

Sally agreed. 'Nothing that looks plain or dark is going to win. Our designs will have to be *really* bright.'

Eric felt miserable. 'What's wrong with the uniform we've got?' he said.

'Nothing,' said Jason. 'But if you want to win those chocolates you've got to forget about that and design a uniform that Mr Peacock will really like.'

Eric went home feeling sad. *Mr Peacock will choose something really bright and totally embarrassing*, he thought, *and it will be our own fault for wanting to win those chocolates so badly. We could end up looking like the kids at Saint Smarty-pants. That would be a disaster.*

The children at Saint Smarty-pants' School had to wear pink and yellow tartan trousers, a green spotted blazer and a red triangular hat with big purple feathers in it.

The children were given a letter to take home.

ST BURGER'S SCHOOL

Dear Parent,

Could YOUR horrid untidy child be a STAR DESIGNER?

Could your little monster design a new uniform for St Burger's School?

If you think they could, tell them to send their drawings to Mr P. Peacock BSc, PGCE, Med, OBE, MAD by Friday.

The best idea will win an ENORMOUS box of chocolates and a photo of your handsome, well-dressed headmaster!

Mr Peacock

Everyone stayed up late that week to work on their designs. They missed television. They missed tea and dinner and supper. They completely forgot about computer games. They were even too busy to argue with their brothers and sisters. Winning the gigantic box of chocolates was all they cared about.

Jason liked cooking, so his uniform had a bright red apron with green pockets and a yellow chef's hat.

Jessie liked space stories, so she designed a shimmering silver suit with solar panels that could power a scooter.

Sally loved scary films, so she thought that vampire teeth and a huge black and purple cape should be part of the uniform.

But Eric was stuck. He couldn't think of one single idea that didn't look silly and embarrassing to wear.

The next assembly was on Thursday and Mr Peacock's orange and red checked suit was so bright that it gave Eric a headache.

'Tomorrow is the final day of the new uniform competition,' Mr Peacock reminded them.

Eric's headache was *very* painful. After assembly he went to ask Mrs Turbot, the school secretary, if he could lie down somewhere. As he waited outside the office he heard voices.

'There are hundreds of entries for the uniform competition,' he heard Mr Peacock say, 'but I hate them all.'

'What? *All* of them?' Mrs Turbot asked.

'Yes. They are far too bright and colourful. I can't possibly allow the children to look more interesting than their handsome, well-dressed headmaster. That would *never* do.'

This gave Eric a brilliant idea. His headache disappeared and he got to work. He handed his entry in to Mrs Turbot just before the competition closed.

On Monday morning Mr Peacock still hadn't found a single uniform design that he liked. Steam was blowing out of his ears and messing up his carefully combed hair.

'These ideas are all terrible,' he said. 'I simply cannot let the children look more colourful than handsome, interesting me.'

He took one last look at the competition entries. They were all very bright because that was what everyone thought he wanted. There were rainbow-coloured uniforms, bright green and red uniforms, lemon yellow, chocolate brown and cherry-coloured uniforms.

There were spacesuits and sailor suits and swimsuits. There were leopard prints and zebra stripes and ideas with feathers all over.

'Wait a minute!' said Mr Peacock, suddenly. 'What's *this*?' He looked at one of the designs more closely, then smiled, then laughed out loud and danced around his office in a very silly way.

'Are you alright, Mr Peacock?' asked Mrs Turbot.

'Yes! I've *found* it! We have a winner!' he shouted.

In assembly, Mr Peacock looked very happy.
'I am *delighted* to tell you,' he said, 'that I have
found our design star.'

Everyone held their breath. They had
dreamed about chocolate all weekend. Mr
Peacock switched on a big projector.

'The winner is ... '

Everyone waited and waited. The tension
was terrible.

'... Eric McDerrick!'

A giant picture of Eric's design came up on the screen. Everyone cheered and clapped because they liked Eric, but nobody understood how his idea could possibly have won.

'It's the same uniform that we have now,' said Jason. 'That doesn't make sense.'

'No, it doesn't,' said Jessie. 'It's exactly the same but with the T-shirt tucked in.'

'But Mr Peacock likes bright colours!' said Sally. 'That's bonkers!'

Mr Peacock shook Eric's hand.

'Here is your magnificent photograph of handsome, well-dressed *me*!' he said.

'Er ... thank you very much,' said Eric politely.

'And here,' Mr Peacock continued, 'is your *enormous* box of extremely expensive chocolates!'

The whole school cheered again.

'But how *did* you win?' asked Jason at playtime.

'Your idea is so plain and ordinary,' said Sally.

'Did you hypnotize him?' asked Jessie.

Eric shook his head and laughed. 'No,' he said. 'I just accidentally found out that Mr Peacock didn't want anyone else's clothes to be brighter than his.'

'Just like a real peacock?' asked Sally.

'Exactly,' said Eric.

And they all nodded.

'At least we won't have to wear anything embarrassing to school now,' said Eric. 'And best of all, there's a massive chocolate-eating party at my house tonight!'

About the author

I grew up in a house near some abandoned allotments. My friends and I spent our holidays climbing trees, building dens and munching on tonnes of fruit. I ate *so many* gooseberries before the age of ten that I could have grown up to be a crumble instead of a writer!

I've done all sorts of jobs, including painting boats and teaching children, but writing funny stories is my *best* and *favourite* thing. I especially love writing stories where kind, clever children are the heroes.

Most grown-ups I know are gentle and friendly, but some – like the adults in this book – are absolutely awful. Luckily, these stories also include boys and girls who are intelligent and brave, and who can sort things out themselves!